Ultimate Power From My Pain

Jemima Nelson

Jemima Nelson

Table of Contents

Dedication

My life would never be what it is without God,

my mother (may her soul rest in peace) and my amazing children;

Kalisha, Donnika, and Alexia Nelson. Not forgetting my awesome grandson, Jeremiah.

I feel blessed and privileged to have such marvellous people.

My mother, Bernice Akua Asabea Azah, was my strength, confidant, and number one fan. She believed in me even when I didn't believe in myself. Mum, I am who I am because of you.

My children and grandson are my worlds. They are the reason for my breath and perseverance every day. I hope to be the role model they need.

This book is dedicated to my three girls and grandson. You can do anything in life when you put your mind to it.

Love always

Jemima

Introduction

Being a full-blown sickle cell sufferer, I understand the disease, how it affects me as a person, and the ways I have managed the symptoms so far. Additionally, I was fortunate to have worked on a sickle cell ward (Haematology and Oncology) when I qualified as a nurse in 2001. At PPW4, a private wing in ULCH, I had the privilege of speaking with numerous sickle cell sufferers and consultants. This experience provided me with a comprehensive insight into the disease, how different people dealt with their crises, the available and effective treatments, and personal views on the disease and life as a whole.

I had a different perception of life and felt more confident in accepting my medical condition, leading me to view life in a completely different way. I can confidently say that my journey began from that point. My self-inspiring phrase *is 'life is too short'* and *'I have no life sentence as a sickle cell sufferer.'* The reasoning behind the latter phrase is that I had the opportunity to care for cancer patients who were given a prognosis of barely two weeks to live, and unfortunately, it often proved to be true. Witnessing patients dying around me due to cancer made me realise that there was nothing to complain about. I have a medical condition, like many others, so why not LIVE LIFE to the fullest?

My main aim is to help fellow sickle cell sufferers understand my journey and why we should be thankful and grateful every day. By doing so, we become stronger daily, achieve more, and focus less on the negatives in our lives and rather on how we can excel despite our challenges. Life must go on.

When you read this book, I hope you can share in my story and be inspired. Sickle cell patients and carriers have looked at me and told me that I've encouraged them. I'm always humbled by that statement because I was simply trying to live my life and not change the world. However, over time, those words and statements have made me believe that I may be doing something right and have the potential to inspire many people like myself.

The next step in my life is to open up to a wider audience by completing my blog page online and my YouTube channel. My aspiration is to make the difference I have been longing for, with the aim of motivating and encouraging others, including caregivers. Each chapter in my book concludes with inspiring phrases to provide encouragement, as well as a list of recommended items that can be purchased from Amazon. These recommendations and links have personally and significantly helped me. I kindly request you to continue following me and sharing in my incredible stories. *My beautiful beginnings*

How it all started - Childhood

My mother and father were carriers of sickle cell, and I was born in Ghana, West Africa. I am a full-blown sickle cell sufferer with SC haemoglobin, inheriting both haemoglobin S and C from both parents. As a child, I frequently visited the hospital due to extreme pain, discomfort, and recurring infections. At the time, I didn't fully comprehend what was happening.

Ironically, I felt blessed to have this condition at the time, as it led to being treated differently. **We are only treated in a certain way because we allow it or permit others to treat us differently.** The worst part for me, and perhaps for other sickle cell sufferers, is when people don't believe the amount of pain we are experiencing or even doubt that we have sickle cell disease. I believe that "the worst kind of disability is the unseen one." This disability causes immense pain, yet not everyone understands how or why. It's difficult to be in excruciating pain but still act as if everything is okay, as society expects. Although one may have certain privileges, strangers often look at us with anger and discomfort because they cannot see our condition and therefore do not understand. When children and spouses are unaware because I'm perceived as managing all the time, it becomes even more challenging. The fact that I may not cry every day and appear to be getting along with life doesn't make it any less difficult.

Sickle cell sufferers do not want to be seen differently, yet we are different. We want to be seen as living everyday lives, but the pain, let me tell you, can be debilitating. Sometimes, one might wish the scale of the pain could be seen across the forehead. It would be nice for someone to experience this pain for a while; why must it be me? Why does one have to act normal and even use distractions to help ease the pain? At times, the desire is to lie down and not wake up, as the pain never disappears.

The pain seems to be there all the time. Even when growing older, my consciousness of the suffering was insurmountable. I tried getting used to the pain – who even does that? It is impossible. It keeps me awake at night and causes me to feel restless, irritable, teary, depressed, helpless, like half-baked Jemima, and many other terrible emotions.

My advice

My coping strategy is to accept this debilitating condition and embrace the fact that I am still alive and here to tell my story. I often tell myself not to feel sorry for myself or helpless. Instead, I strive to build courage, recognising that we are all unique and wonderfully made. I harness the power of my mind

to believe that I am not different; I am just like anyone else. Your mind is powerful, so feed it with positive thoughts, and you are already a winner.

"To be happy is the purpose of our lives"

Dalai Lama

What The Fuss Is All About

People with sickle cell anaemia acquire the condition from their biological parents. In sickle cell anaemia, the gene responsible for generating normal red blood cells undergoes mutation or alteration. Individuals who inherit the faulty haemoglobin protein gene from both biological parents develop sickle cell anaemia. Those who inherit the mutant gene from one biological parent exhibit sickle cell characteristics.

Mutation unquestionably affects red blood cells.

Haemoglobin, found in the normal red blood cell, is a protein. During haemoglobin mutation, sickled cells are created. Unfortunately, this cannot navigate throughout your circulatory system properly and, therefore cannot transport oxygen, essential nutrients, and even hormones throughout your body.

Normal haemoglobin is soluble, unlike abnormal haemoglobin, which forms clumps because it cannot dissolve.

Red blood cells must be flexible to squeeze and slide through small blood channels. Red blood cells bearing aberrant stable haemoglobin can't accomplish that. Instead, blood cells with defective haemoglobin obstruct blood arteries and blood flow.Normal red blood cells last roughly 120 days. Sickled cells self-destruct after 10 to 20 days. Usually, the bone marrow is responsible for producing an adequate number of red blood cells to replenish the ones that have died. However, in cases where cell death occurs more frequently than usual, the bone marrow works overtime to match the body's demand for new red blood cells. If the bone marrow is unable to maintain the required production, it will result in a shortage of red blood cells.

Sickle cell anaemia symptoms often emerge when babies are 5 to 6 months old. As individuals with sickle cell anaemia grow older, they face an increased risk of developing other medical disorders, some of which can be life-threatening. However, by being aware of these diseases and their symptoms, individuals with sickle cell anaemia can seek treatment at the earliest indication of trouble, allowing healthcare experts to provide appropriate care for the condition.

Healthcare providers may refer to this situation as an acute pain crisis. Vaso-occlusive crisis (VOC), also known as acute pain crises, is the most common reason why sickle cell anaemia patients seek emergency room care or require hospitalisation. Symptoms include:

- Sudden severe ache.

- Pain might be sharp or stabbing.

- VOC may affect any body region but generally affects your abdomen, lower back, arms, and legs.

Living with VOC is one of the more challenging elements of having sickle cell anaemia.

My advice

Educate yourself about the condition: what it entails, how to manage its symptoms, what to expect in terms of living with a disability, and how it may impact different stages of your life. This includes understanding the choices and decisions you may need to make, such as selecting a life partner, deciding on having children and exploring available options. Knowledge is crucial, so don't be caught off guard. Ask questions, engage with support groups, and meet like-minded individuals.

"Education is the most powerful weapon which you can use to change the world."

Nelson Mandela

Stigma and the not-so-fun side of Sickle Cell

Healthcare workers sometimes call VOC 'the invisible sickness' because patients with a pain crisis often don't have symptoms other than sudden severe pain that's only eased with opioid pills. Along with other symptoms and issues, persons with sickle cell anaemia may experience anxiety or sadness due to stigmas associated with the condition.

According to studies, people's need for opiate medications to reduce VOC is correlated with the stigma associated with sickle cell anaemia. I can attest to having also been a victim. While on the ward, I overheard nurses referring to sickle cell patients as drug addicts during handover. This was frustrating to hear as they were aware I suffer from the disease; it seemed they either didn't care if I heard it or had become accustomed to using such terms and forgot that I was present in the room.

According to other research, individuals of colour are less likely to be prescribed painkillers and must wait longer to receive them compared to white individuals. It is understandable why this research produced those results. The stigma was real, and being given regular painkillers meant they were encouraging what they perceived as our addiction. Given that sickle cell anaemia frequently affects Black or Hispanic people, these stigmas combine to provide a devastating one-two punch. I have had arguments with various nurses during some of my hospital admissions, explaining to them that I have all the opioids needed to get high at home without having to come into the hospital. Why would I leave the comfort of my home just to come to the hospital and be high? I come to the hospital because the pain becomes unbearable, and the intravenous infusion and a PCA or alternative to help ease the pain from the hospital would be beneficial. More so, staying in the hospital for more than 2 days is not feasible as I have family and a business to run. But even with that knowledge and explanation, they still treated me as if I only came to be drugged up. As a nurse, and worse, as a previous haematology nurse, I couldn't believe I was being treated like that. Its always been my objective to give my best while working on the wards, and now that I need someone to look after me, it feels like I'm bothering the nurses.

Below are some important facets of sickle cell you should look out for; I am glad I learned about them whilst working on the haematology ward.

Acute chest syndrome (ACS)

Acute chest syndrome, a symptom of sickle cell anaemia, which accounts for most hospital admission and, ultimately, death. ACS occurs when sickled cells form clusters and obstruct blood arteries in the lungs.

Symptoms include:

- Sudden chest discomfort.

- Coughing.

- High temperature.

- Shortness of breath.

Anaemia

People with sickle cell anaemia may have mild, moderate, or severe forms of anaemia. **Possible symptoms are:**

- Pale skin colour.

- Fatigue.

- Shortness of breath.

- Heart palpitations

Additionally, newborns suffering from anaemia may be extraordinarily fussy or tetchy. Growth in children may be reduced or may approach puberty later than colleagues.

Newborn screening

In England, screening for sickle cell disease is offered as part of the newborn blood spot heel prick test at birth. This practice was implemented in the UK between 2003 and 2006.

In Ghana, an estimated 18,000 babies (out of a total of 896,000 births) are born each year with sickle cell disease. Newborn screening was initiated in 1993 but was initially limited to the Greater Accra and Ashanti regions. However, since 2021, the screening program has been expanded to improve early diagnosis and reduce the number of deaths in children under the age of 5 and emergency admissions among children with undiagnosed sickle cell disease.

In Nigeria, newborn screening programmes are also being expanded and developed.

Antenatal screening

All pregnant women in England are offered a blood test to determine if they carry a gene for thalassaemia. Those who are at high risk of being carriers for sickle cell disease are offered a test for sickle cell. This test should ideally be conducted before 10 weeks of pregnancy, as early testing is crucial. If you discover that you are a carrier, you and your partner will have the option to undergo additional tests to determine if your baby will be affected by the condition. In cases where both parents are carriers for sickle cell or thalassaemia, there are two tests available to assess whether the baby will be affected.

Chorionic villus sampling (CVS)

This procedure is typically conducted between 11 and 14 weeks of pregnancy. A fine needle is typically inserted through the mother's abdomen to collect a small tissue sample from the placenta. The cells extracted from the tissue can then be tested for sickle cell disease or thalassaemia.

Amniocentesis

This procedure is performed at 15 weeks of pregnancy. A fine needle is inserted through the mother's abdomen into the uterus to obtain a small sample of the fluid surrounding the baby. The fluid contains some of the baby's cells, which can be tested for sickle cell disease or thalassemia.

Pre-implantation genetic diagnosis for sickle cell disease

Using a process similar to IVF, the fertilised embryo is genetically tested for sickle cell disease. If the embryo is unaffected, it is then implanted. This procedure is currently only available in some specialised centres in England.

Stroke

Babies and adults with sickle cell anaemia are both at risk for stroke. Research shows that by the age of 20, 11% of patients with sickle cell anaemia may develop strokes, and that figure increases to 24% within 25 years.

Some stroke symptoms to look out for:

- Severe headache.

- You suddenly feel weaker on one side of your body.

- Change in attentiveness.

- Difficulty in Speaking.

- Vision problems.

- Mobility issues

Splenetic Sequestration Crises

It occurs when sickled-shaped cells are caught in the spleen, expanding your spleen. Thus causing acute anaemia as there is a huge drop in haemoglobin. This can be life-threatening, and usually, splenectomy is considered if there has been more than one occurrence.

Symptoms include:

- Pain in your upper left tummy (abdomen).

- Weakness

- Paleness,

- Palpitations

- Unusual feeling of sleeping

Bacterial infections

Streptococcus pneumoniae, Haemophilus influenzae, and non-Typhi Salmonella species are the main causes of infection in sickle cell sufferers.

Symptoms include

- High temperature

- Coughing

- Shortness of breath

- Painful joints

- Headaches

Leg ulcers

Sickle cell patients also commonly develop leg ulcers, typically starting from the age of 10. Leg ulcers can occur at any stage in the life of a sickle cell sufferer, and they experience painful symptoms that often do not heal. It usually begins with lesions on their ankles. During my time working on the haematology ward, this was a frequent occurrence, and I cared for a lady who had extensive ulcers affecting both legs. Unfortunately, her ulcers never healed, and she passed away one afternoon while in the ward. Currently, a friend of mine is suffering from similar ulcers on both legs, and I always remember her in my prayers, hoping for God's healing power to intervene.

Priapism

Research shows that 35% of male sickle cell anaemia sufferers experience priapism, which is characterised by painful erections that can last for up to four hours or even longer. I came across this term when a friend asked me a question: 'My son has had an erection for 2 hours; could it be related to his condition?' Curious, I conducted some research and discovered that priapism is indeed a symptom of sickle cell anaemia. It occurs when blood remains trapped in the penis and fails to drain properly due to the presence of abnormal cells. If left untreated, it can lead to permanent and irreversible damage to the delicate penile tissue. To relieve this condition, warm water baths are recommended to improve circulation and alleviate the painful symptoms. Ice packs can also be used to reduce swelling and promote blood drainage. In some cases, surgery may be necessary to provide relief for the sufferer.

Pulmonary hypertension (PH)

Sickle cell sufferers are known to suffer from PH (when the pressure is high in the pulmonary arteries.)

Symptoms include:

- Racing pulse.

- Fainting (passing out) or dizziness.

- Feeling short of breath during exercise or activity and difficulty breathing even at rest.

Chronic kidney disease

It is also known that sickle cell sufferers develop chronic renal dysfunction.

Symptoms include:

- Urge to urinate more often.

- Reduced appetite.

- Enlarged hands, feet, and ankles.

- Breathlessness.

- Blood in urine or looks frothy.

- Puffed-up eyes.

- Dry and itchy skin (pruritus).

- Trouble concentrating.

- Reduced sleep.

- Nausea or vomiting.

- Muscle cramping.

- Hypertension.

Detached retina

The retinas can be detached due to the sickled cells obstructing blood arteries in your retinas. I have to have an annual eye test at the hospital as a precautionary measure. So far I am good. Thank God!

Common symptoms include:

- Seeing flashes of light.

- Seeing many floaters — specks, threads, dark spots, and squiggly lines that drift across your vision. (Seeing a few here and there is typical and does not cause panic.)

- Your side vision (peripheral vision) becomes darker.

- Darkening or shadow obscuring part of your view.

Bone pain is a trademark symptom of sickle cell disease (SCD) and affects almost all individuals with sickle cell at some point. It can be either localised or diffuse. The pain is often described as a deep, dull ache and is intensified by movement or pressure. I can certainly attest to this, as mentioned earlier. It feels like someone is trying to extract my bone marrow, indicating profound pain. Most adolescents and adults with sickle cell anaemia experience chronic pain. As I age and face the stresses of life, my pain seems to persist constantly. During an MRI scan conducted due to the pain, the doctors informed me that I had developed necrosis in my right hip bone. Indeed, it's always excruciating when sitting for extended periods or remaining in one position for a prolonged time.

The pain can be so severe that it interferes with my daily activities, such as walking, standing, or sitting, leading to disability and decreased quality of life. This chronic pain normally manifests in the hips, knees, ankles, wrists, elbows, and shoulders. Mine is mainly in my hip and elbows. Occasionally my chest, but now my hips are beginning to suffer too.

My advice

Listen to your body, and don't push yourself too much. I try and do as I preach, but sometimes it is impossible. Take your follow-up appointments seriously. If you miss an appointment, please rebook. Prevention is always better than cure. Due to the numerous tasks I have to manage and the natural effects of ageing, I have become exceptionally forgetful nowadays. As a result, I make it a point to write things down and rely on reminders and alarms set on my phone, in my diary, on the fridge, and even on my computer. Please do what works best for you.

"It is often the small steps, not the giant leaps, that bring about the most lasting change."

HRM Queen Elizbeth II

The Patient. The Mother. The Entrepreneur

Suppose you have a copy of this book. You may be a sickle cell sufferer, a parent of a sickle cell sufferer, a professional, or someone who knows someone suffering from sickle cell. Perhaps you're interested out of curiosity, or maybe you're a complete novice on the subject. In any case, I will focus on the latter audience mentioned above.

Sickle cell disease is a hereditary disorder affecting millions worldwide, primarily those of African descent. The disease causes red blood cells to form an abnormal crescent shape, leading to chronic pain, organ damage, and a shortened lifespan. Sickle cell is inherited, and any haemoglobin apart from the A genotype is considered disabled. To provide a better understanding, let me explain with an example.

My mother is a carrier of the AC genotype, and my father has the AS genotype. My mother contributed the C gene, and my father contributed the S gene, resulting in my combined genotype of SC. My sister, Patricia Biney, inherited the S gene from our father and the A gene from our mother, making her a sickle cell carrier with the AS genotype (also known as a trait carrier). The fortunate sibling is my brother, Daniel Phillips, who inherited the A genotype from both parents, making him a non-sickle cell carrier with the AA genotype, considered an average individual. Patricia is somewhat fortunate, but it means that if her husband, Mr. Kofi Biney, were a carrier or a sickle cell patient, their children might be carriers or suffer from sickle cell disease. Luckily, Kofi does not carry the sickle cell gene, and the rest is practically history.

Now you may understand why I consider Daniel to be so fortunate. His genotype allows him to freely choose his partner without concerns about their genotypes. Although it may sound like promoting incest, it's just a way of emphasising the point. On the other hand, as a full-blown sickle cell patient, the chances of me having a child with sickle cell disease are 75%, and there is a 25% chance of having a child who is a carrier of the gene. Unfortunately, I will never have the opportunity to have a child without sickle cell disease. This poses a significant challenge for many sickle cell patients as they reach childbearing age or even before.

I cannot speak for people in this position as I was fortunate that the children would either be AC or AS as their dad was not a carrier. I just had to wait till they were born to test their genotype to know which one they inherited. My most painful age was when I was ready to have children. I say this because you do not try or ask someone for their genotype before you fall in love. Unfortunately, it is the opposite; you fall in love, then ask them, "Ohhh, by the way, I suffer from sickle cell," To be honest, sometimes you never even want to bring that up for fear of the unknown. Would he stay or leave? Would his family agree for us to date/marry, and would my children suffer as much as I have? This latter statement is aimed at sickle cell patients. As a carrier, one may not experience any pain or discomfort.

Ignorance about the disease means we have relationships with no expectations or planning. The truth hits home when the child is born, or the nurse advises you to have an amniocentesis procedure. Amniocentesis is a test that may be provided to you during pregnancy to determine whether your unborn child has a chromosomal or genetic disorder, according to the National Health Services (NHS).

When this procedure is recommended, I believe these thoughts may run through one's mind – as they did for me when it was suggested to my oldest daughter. Also, I have had other sickle cell sufferers like me made some of the statements below when I used to work as a Haematology nurse at the University College London Hospital (UCLH)

"This procedure can be dangerous to both mother and child."

"That is when all sorts of emotions run in your mind."

"Why did I not ask my partner before we got involved."

"Why did we both not test before the pregnancy."

"Should I ignore the professional and see what happens after the baby."

"Maybe, as we have just discovered we are both sickle cell carriers, it would be best not to have children at all."

"I do not want to have a sickle cell child."

Currently, technology has developed to incredible lengths, including medical intervention. Although there is no preventative development, there are more amazing interventions in the USA than in the UK. There is a stem cell transplant which is the ultimate cure for sickle cell if all goes well. There are other options, such as artificial insemination, egg harvest collection, and Crispr Gene DNA editing which has been used in some parts of Africa, namely Ghana. As mentioned, there is amniocentesis to check the baby's genotype during pregnancy. As a Christian, my belief is definitely against the last procedure. Before anyone becomes judgmental, I would like to explain.

As a sickle cell sufferer, I am so grateful my parents weren't given that option. I never asked them and would not want to put my mum in that position. But you should consider what would have happened if that was an option in the 1970s. No Jemima

Nelson, and possibly no other excellent human beings, sickle cell sufferers would have been born. How would this world survive without me? [just a bit of my not-so-funny humour?]

The initial myths about sickle cell sufferers are almost a thing of the past. Some of the tales familiar during my upbringing included:

Sickle cell sufferers would die before turning 18.

Sickle cell sufferers won't be able to have children.

Keeping a job would be difficult.

Sickle cell sufferers would be in pain until death.

Sickle cell sufferers would have sickle cell children.

They would not be able to have children due to complications.

They would always have blood transfusions during pregnancy.

It would be impossible for them to pursue their education due to pain, fatigue, or crises.

They would definitely suffer from chronic and incurable ulcers due to the condition.

They could never be in a long-term or loving relationship.

The list could go on to a few more pages if I remember everything I have been told or read about regarding sickle cell.

I am proof that every statement above does not apply to every sickle cell sufferer. Almost all the ideas mentioned above can happen to anyone with a medical condition, including sickle cell sufferers. It should not be worn around any sickle cell sufferer's neck as if it is our birth-right. I can categorically say that I am an almost 50-year-old sickle cell sufferer, a mother of three beautiful and unique girls, Kalisha, Donnika, and Alexia Nelson, and a grandmother to a remarkable young, energetic boy, Jeremiah—a divorcee, A CEO of a Travel and Occupational Health (OH) clinic since 2007. I qualified as a nurse in 2001 with a diploma, then attained a degree in Occupational Health and furthered my career by obtaining an MBA in 2021. Sickle cell is not a deterrent to achieving a lot in life.

In 2007, I decided to start working for myself as my employers at that time did not consider my sickle cell in any way. I was a qualified OHA, and my employers didn't care at all when I was pregnant with my last daughter. I only had an hour's relief by another staff member when I went for my NHS appointments, very laughable; this even caused more stress in life and therefore triggered more crises. After my maternity, I started the business. It was daunting at first, but I ignored all the negative advice and discouragement. I had an amazing father-in-law who urged me on and encouraged me.

It was worrisome that my health would affect my work and vice versa, but even though I was undertaking a new venture, I wasn't overwhelmed. I was determined to make it work, and it did. The business has been running for 13 years now. It was through hard work, dedication, and perseverance. I worked tirelessly every day and even had another branch in Leicester (which closed due to COVID). I was so determined to keep this business going and also distract myself from the constant pain that I even worked during my admissions. My consultant and nurses always told me off when I was on my laptop on the ward, but I knew it kept me going. I didn't focus on the pain. I felt like I was achieving something in life. Being a business owner comes with its challenges and positive sides, but being a sickle cell sufferer makes it even harder. As you are aware, stress and strenuous work can trigger my crises, but I always challenge myself. I like to win and would do anything to win, sickle cell or not.

It's always been my belief that I can do anything if I put my mind to it. "No one should get it twisted" is a statement I hear from my girls. I am not trivialising sickle cell disease at all. I suffer from excruciating chronic pain; when I mean pain, I mean

PAIN. Most times, rating the pain out of 10 would be a 15. However, my view of life is not to let my condition, situation, or discomfort limit me. I would work, learn and achieve in pain if I had to; just visualising my goal means that I look past my situation and aim for a good and fantastic future, just like anyone. Why should I feel different? Why should I not succeed? Why should I fail because of my disability and society's perception of me?

My advice

To the adolescents and young adults, I know you cannot help who you fall in love with, but please get yourself tested for sickle cell now. It is worth knowing your partner's genotype too. **Know Your Genotype.** But if you do have a child who is a sickle cell sufferer, trust me, it is not the end of the world. I am a living testimony.

There are other ways to test your unborn child or still even using IVF if you would prefer to go down that line.

"Not how long, but how well you have lived is the main thing."

Seneca

The Cries in Crisis

I was born in Ghana, West Africa, on 11th August 1973. I stayed in Ghana till I was 19 years of age, where I travelled to the United Kingdom. This was supposed to be a two-week holiday before returning to start my pharmacist degree at a University in Ghana. Well, I managed to convince my dad I would be right back before he even knew it, and 30 years later, I am still here. I found out I suffered from sickle cell at a very early age, I cannot remember the exact age, but I remember I had to go to the hospital many times as a child. My dad got me numerous books about Sickle Cell Disease. I remember he got me a giant book that I read religiously as it answered many of my questions about sickle cell, why I was different from my siblings, why I was always in pain, and how I would cope with the disease. I do not think it was the best, as the world has rapidly evolved since then. Well, well, well, where do I start? I need to do a little 'thank you, Jesus' dance. That book taught me that ....

I am more likely to die by age 18, a maximum of 21 years.

I may not be able to have children.

My life will be different from everyone else because of my condition.

I may develop organ failures.

I may need regular blood transfusions.

And a lot more.

Can you imagine how I felt as a young girl growing up knowing all these things? A death sentence before I could even start living. An impossible start to life. If you know me well, this is where the phrase "Life is too short" was generated.

While growing up, I always knew I would die before the age of 21 years; what a life! Why was I even here?

What is the point? Why all this suffering? I never was a girly child and didn't bother with dolls that much; what did it matter if I wasn't going to live long enough to have my children? I cannot remember much of what I used to think about then; all I knew was I would enjoy life to the fullest. Nothing would stand in my way even if I didn't make it to 21. "Sickle cell or no sickle cell," for me, life was too short, and I was going to make the best of however little time I had on earth.

Although I felt pain most times, especially during certain times, days, and events, I sometimes believed the pain was more severe on some days than others. I could not understand why. I later learned of the triggers of my condition, which included infection, stress (no wonder I was experiencing more crises often during my exams), extreme temperature, and dehydration. I describe my pain as trying to extract my bone marrow without anaesthetics. The pain is sometimes so unbearable I feel I could do without those limbs - mainly my knees and elbows.

As a child, I did not know any different; I thought whatever I was going through was normal. My siblings made me feel that I was slightly different as they were hardly unwell—they never complained as much as I did and looked healthier than me (I could be assuming this statement as I was the skinniest sibling, which meant I was not fit). My health was not the best, but my mental strength was incredible as a teenager.

Although sickle cell is a disease predominantly found in individuals of African descent and one that originated in Africa, I have often pondered how I managed to survive in Ghana, given the quality of treatment I am currently receiving in the United Kingdom (UK). This thought arises from my childhood experiences while growing up in Ghana, particularly during my visits to Korle Bu Hospital, the primary hospital in the country, which were nothing short of dreadful.

There were no beds, long waiting times, sometimes waiting for hours to be seen, no medication, and family members had to donate blood before a blood transfusion was given. I remember sad and traumatising admissions. However, there were private hospitals such as Osu RE Hospital, Ridge Hospital, etc. Korle Bu Hospital was known as a teaching and renowned hospital with the best doctors in Accra (the capital of Ghana). On one of my admissions at Korle Bu, I was given a bed to lie down on due to sickle cell; my pain was unbearable. As we waited for the nurse to attend to me, I heard someone screaming in agony while being pushed in a wheelchair towards my mom and me. When he got closer, we realised it was a boy suffering from a sickle cell crisis. I was asked to get off the bed as his pain was more severe than mine. So, I reluctantly climbed off the bed, and the boy was placed on it. After approximately 30 minutes, he died. I was then asked to lie on the bed.

Honestly, I cannot even remember if the sheet was changed; this was in the 70s. OMG, my pain instantly disappeared. I was so overwhelmed with grief and fear that I thought the same would happen if I lay on the bed. I quietly told my mom I wanted to go home, with tears in my eyes and shaking with fear. All of this happened right in front of me. For years, I could not get the image out of my head. Imagine how traumatised I was as a child. But as a teenager, my life was not too bad; it is evident from the previous chapters that I did enjoy those years. I struggled with exams because I used to get very stressed, which triggered my crises.

I studied science as I always wanted to be in the medical

field, a pharmacist, to be precise. I have always wanted to contribute to humanity and help others suffering like me.

I always wanted to be a typical teenager, but my mom was overprotective. I wanted to go out like my friends and sneak into parties and nightclubs, but I couldn't do that because I was often in excruciating pain. Sometimes I hid my feelings because I used to think I was complaining too much. Like most of us, I blamed myself a lot. I'm sure I even lost friends during that time in my life. I am very emotional, and I believe it all stemmed from my condition and how I couldn't be as normal as others. Chronic pain, this invisible disability, can be frustrating as many may assume I am lazy or a chronic complainer. I was sometimes bitter, angry, and tearful, and I just pitied myself for the pain I was experiencing.

My young adult life took an unexpected turn as I was supposed to go to university after passing my A-levels in Ghana, which was both my parents' and sometimes my own wish. However, during my holidays, I reconnected with an old friend in the United Kingdom. She shared stories of her extraordinary life, working in the UK while attending university. That idea sparked something within me, and it started to grow and take root. I began contemplating the best plan I could devise to make my way to the United Kingdom or possibly the United States of America. At that moment, I had temporarily forgotten about my sickle cell condition and the challenges it could pose in a foreign country without my parents. I was determined to fight for my independence.

After much strategic planning and several modifications to the original plan, I heard that my dad would be travelling to the UK soon. I seized the opportunity and managed to convince him that we should travel together, suggesting it would give me a chance to see the UK and take a break before university. Eventually, he agreed to buy the ticket for me after I had applied for the visa. Deep down, I could sense that he was secretly hoping I wouldn't obtain the visa, perhaps to avoid any blame if I couldn't travel. At the time, my dad owned a home in Neasden, UK.

However, he kept saying that life in the UK was too complicated and stressful and that he never wanted to live here. He would quickly discourage any idea of working or living in the UK. With determination and perseverance, I arrived in the UK two months before my 20th birthday. It was the most fantastic time of my life because I experienced freedom for the first time. I could do whatever I liked, I felt more like an adult, and I knew that the sky was the limit. I had no intention of adhering to the plan I had presented to my dad; fortunately, I was now in control of my life and the path I truly desired.

My advice

Take chances; don't let your condition define you. Enjoy the journey, and don't wait until you reach the destination. My great and not-so-great experiences have shaped me into who I am today. Sickle cell disease shouldn't hinder you from living life. Be free, but be careful and always remember the triggers of sickle cell and try to avoid them if possible. Avoid smoking and reduce or eliminate alcohol consumption. Take precautions to prevent infections and strive to maintain a stress-free lifestyle. Additionally, avoid extreme weather conditions, or if unavoidable, manage your expectations accordingly. Do the best you can!

"The big lesson in life, baby, is never to be scared of anyone or anything."

Frank Sinatra

The brains behind the beauty

During my secondary school years, I never felt like I was in a boarding house. Both of my parents would visit every Saturday without fail. My mom would bring the best home-cooked meal, while my dad would bring biscuits, drinks, and provisions. I'm certain that some of my colleagues envied me because some of them didn't receive any visits for months. It's hard to imagine how I used to feel in school; at times, I even forgot that I had a disability. Perhaps, playing devil's advocate, their regular visits were their way of compensating for the pain I was going through.

My house teacher and all the relevant parties were aware that I suffered from sickle cell disease and could experience a crisis at any moment. Initially, I wasn't keen on everyone knowing about my condition. However, sometimes certain misfortunes can be a blessing, as now I was classified as a teenager with special needs. I received careful treatment, and detailed attention was given to me most of the time.

Again, to give you an idea of how blessed I was during my teenage years, in the boarding house, we had to wake up very early and go down a hill in Accra Girls to fetch water (icy water) for bathing. If you ever heard someone screaming in the bathroom, it would be me whenever I poured water on myself.

Strangely enough, I actually enjoyed it. Being a sickle cell sufferer had its advantages, as it allowed me to have some privileges. My parents intervened, and I was permitted to use portable water heaters to warm my water before bathing. It was truly a blessing. Moreover, due to my condition, I could go home more frequently than the average student. If you could see me now, I would have both hands in the air, signalling the sickle cell emojis. At one point, my friends at school started to wonder whether I was a boarding student or a day student, considering how often I went home.

I realised I couldn't have my cake and eat it too; I didn't want to be known as the girl with sickle cell disease, but I wanted the perks associated with the condition. I was determined to study and make it in life. Education is key, which I constantly tell my girls. Science was my favourite subject as I was always curious about nature and life. I was initially fascinated by the human body, and due to my overzealous urge to always win, I also enjoyed solving problems. So, taking physics, chemistry, and biology in sixth form formed the basis of my professional career. However, being a pharmacist was my preferred occupation.

Providing services and helping people have always been my passion. Although I didn't become a pharmacist, I still managed to enter the health arena and offer assistance where it was needed. Personally, I evaluate myself as determined, persevering, and committed to getting the job done. Don't get me wrong; I have faced my fair share of challenges and disappointments. However, being a CEO has been the best thing that has ever happened to me. It feels like having a permanent job that encompasses everyone's responsibilities.

My advice

Never see yourself as different from others. My encouraging phrase here is, 'I can do what anyone can do, and sometimes even better.' Nothing will deter me, as I find joy in achieving goals. Set both short-term and long-term goals for yourself. These goals can be in any area of life, and as you achieve them, you will gain confidence. Remember that little drops of water make a mighty ocean. If some of your goals are taking longer to achieve, don't hesitate. As long as you keep moving, whether it's crawling, jogging, or running, it is certainly an achievement. Just remember not to be stagnant. Keep moving forward, have faith, and persevere. The light at the end of the tunnel may just appear brighter with each passing day.

"The way I see it, if you want the rainbow, you gotta put up with the rain."

Dolly Parton

Miracles in my life

I got a job at Sainsbury's when my Kalisha was just 1. I was a single mother and struggling. I worked as a cashier, but life was challenging with my condition, working a permanent job, and looking after a small child. While working there, I met my most fantastic guardian angel, Nancy Stewart. She has held my hand from that point until now. I always served her when she came to shop at Sainsbury's, Nine Elms. Although she knew I was an immigrant, she offered to help and has never stopped supporting me. She is heaven-sent. When she first took my number and said she would call, I doubted that she would; as a middle-class, wealthy white woman, my initial thought was, why me? Why would she want to help a stranger, someone burdened by all the problems and limitations imposed by nature? Why would she want to help me? When Sainsbury's sacked me for something I didn't do, Nancy stood by me until I was reinstated to the same branch and checkout. Imagine what was going through my head - no job, single mother, sickle cell sufferer, etc. But my good Lord is always on my side.

But as a Christian, I also believe that God works miraculously, and help is consistently delivered through people and other forms on this earth. It was evident to me that my redeemer lived when she contacted me, and from that point on, my life began to change drastically for the better. Nancy supported me in applying for access to Nursing and remained by my side throughout my educational journey. She was always there for me when I needed her help or expert advice and continued to support me until I qualified as a registered nurse. However, my luck and blessings did not end there. I was fortunate enough to secure employment on a Haematology and Oncology ward when my stay in the UK was finalised. UCLH applied to the Home Office on my behalf, and finally, I gained the ability to work and travel in the UK without any restrictions.

Another one of my angels on earth was Dominic McHugh, an optometrist at Kings College Hospital. Our friendship began when I was referred to him for a routine check, and he learned about my struggles with sickle cell, being a single mother, and my pursuit of a nursing career. He generously offered his support throughout my nursing studies, truly a Godsend.

Despite my medical condition, I was very confident, and my determination never wavered. While working at Sainsbury's, God sent another angel, Akosua Baah, a mother, a confidant, and my prayer warrior, who also believed in me. We both worked as cashiers on the tills. She is also from Ghana and took to me instantly. As a Christian and an extraordinary woman, she always felt she had to help me. Those years were the most challenging of my life. I had no immediate family in the UK to support me, but her family helped look after Kalisha when I had to work. I gained two beautiful younger sisters, Adjoa Baah (now Mrs. Phillips), who ironically married my nephew, and her sister, Bena Baah. Akosua provided for Kalisha and me; she would cook, encourage, and pray with me — these fundamental necessities of life that I desperately needed.

She also introduced me to Living Flames Baptist Church, UK. I was blessed with my godly parents, Bishop Eric and Lady Lucy Ntorinkansah, the founders of the church. They guided me through life challenges as a young single mother. I fellowshipped at their church until I met the father of my children. Bishop Eric blessed my marriage in 2002 and oversaw our tenth anniversary in 2012. Living Church was where my Christian life began. Little did I know that God was preparing me for even more incredible and better things through it all. I have truly lived a fulfilling life.

While I was studying nursing at South Bank, God blessed me with another angel, Sheelagh Mealing. She was my personal tutor and became a friend to my family. She guided me throughout my three-year study and truly felt like a divine gift. Interestingly, during one of her visits to our house, she presented us with her family photo album. To my surprise, the album had my birth date written on the first page: 11th August 1973. Overwhelmed with emotion, I asked her why that date, and she revealed that it was her marriage anniversary. As fate would have it, she would celebrate 50 years of marriage on the same day that I turned 50. What are the odds? It then became clear to me that she was always meant to be a part of my life.

Then, when we moved to Surrey, I met another amazing person named Mary Clarke. She was my sickle cell consultant (currently retired) and a great individual. She is the reason why this book is available on Amazon and in various households. Mary believed in me more than I believed in myself; she always encouraged me to write this book to inspire other sickle cell sufferers. I am blessed and will always be indebted to all the wonderful people mentioned above, as well as those I may not have mentioned. May God bless all my friends, family, acquaintances, and even my enemies for shaping me into the person I am today.

My advice

Always have people in your life who encourage and support you. As human beings, we are not meant to survive alone. Having all these amazing people in my life gave me hope. I learned different life skills from all these special individuals mentioned above. We need people who believe in us despite our shortcomings; they make us invincible and drive us to achieve more in life. Seek out individuals who believe in you, whether they are family members, professionals, or even strangers.

A positive mindset can benefit individuals with sickle cell disease. It can help them cope with pain, improve their mental health, increase resilience, and enhance their overall quality of life. Healthcare providers and loved ones can support sickle cell patients in developing a positive mindset by providing emotional support and encouraging them to focus on the positive aspects of their lives.

Don't bear this burden alone; share, destress, and offload onto the appropriate people when needed. Not everyone will be suitable, as some individuals may exacerbate your symptoms. Choose wisely and always maintain a positive mindset.

"To write about life first, you must live it."

Ernest Hemingway.

Ghana vs UK, the mindset beats it all.

Life in the UK was not initially what I expected. I didn't realise that I needed to obtain an NI (National Insurance) number to work, and I was unaware that I would have to pay rent. Additionally, I conveniently forgot about the various bills that come with being independent. Moreover, the most concerning aspect was the extreme and unpredictable weather. I soon discovered that sickle cell disease and snow are a terrible combination, but I reassured myself by recalling that I had managed extreme heat in Ghana, so hopefully, I would be fine. However, I swiftly adapted to life in the UK and quickly learned my way around things.

My dream was starting to waver beneath my feet. I realised I couldn't stay with my cousin for too long. Nothing is free in the UK, and even if it were, it wouldn't last. Reality hit me, and I began searching for accommodation because my cousin's crowded house couldn't accommodate me for much longer. Her aunt, the owner of the house, visited frequently, but she was away for work, or so I was told when I arrived. I was becoming a burden. Eventually, I moved in with a friend I met through my cousin. It was short-lived but worthwhile, as I quickly realised that living with a non-family member or a stranger can take a toll when you aren't contributing significantly to their finances.

During my first year in the UK, I noticed that although I still experienced sickle cell crises, the frequency of my pain had decreased. I was thrilled about my independence and, as a result, paid less attention to my pain.

Having sickle cell has not been the best, but living in the UK was supposed to be better than living in Ghana. There is a myth that sickle cell patients cannot have malaria.

To enlighten some readers, sickle cell is caused by a gene mutation related to malaria. Mosquitoes deposit the parasite into our round blood cells. However, due to the gene mutation, mosquitoes are unable to perform this operation with the crescent-shaped cells. The fact is that we can suffer from malaria, and it can be extremely detrimental to our health when we do. I can personally attest to a day when I thought I would die from malaria. I contracted malaria, and it was a severe experience. Unfortunately, this is the reality. For a sickle cell patient, contracting malaria can be a life-and-death situation. Living in the UK, where mosquitoes are not present, I feel that I can achieve a better life without fearing death from malaria.

I received my first council flat when Kalisha was 1 year old. This helped boost my confidence and even made me believe I could achieve better and greater things. Initially, I was given emergency accommodation at Peckham, then a temporary 1-

bedroom flat at Camberwell until I was finally moved to a 2-bedroom maisonette in Walworth, Latimer House.

Finally, life in the UK is improving day by day. I have my own house with a garden, and even better, my flat is just a bus ride away from Kings College Hospital, where I receive all my medical care. Kalisha got a nursery near our home, and my life is slowly falling into place. I am determined to create a good life for my child and myself. I refuse to let myself become my own enemy.

Being in the UK has had a positive impact on my life, such as improved access to specialist care, education, and awareness. I have attended a few awareness courses in my life.

Regular health checks: Regular health checks can help identify and manage complications of sickle cell disease, such as infections, anaemia, and organ damage. Sickle cell sufferers should receive regular health checks from their healthcare providers to monitor their condition and manage complications.

Access to pain management: Sickle cell disease can cause severe pain, which can be challenging to manage. Patients should have access to effective pain management, including medications and non-pharmacological approaches, to help relieve their pain and improve their quality of life.

Research and development of new treatments: There is a need for continued research and development of new therapies for sickle cell disease. The UK government and private organisations should invest in research to identify new treatment options for sickle cell sufferers. Sickle cell disease is a significant health problem for people of African and African-Caribbean descent in the UK. To provide better treatment for sickle cell sufferers, there needs to be improved access to specialist care, education, awareness programs, regular health checks, access to pain management, and continued research and development of new treatments. I have the best of both worlds, being a sickle cell sufferer and having the privilege to work as a sickle cell nurse for almost six years.

Having a positive mindset can have many benefits for sickle cell sufferers. Here are some of how a positive attitude can be helpful:

Coping with pain: Sickle cell disease can cause severe pain, which can be challenging to manage. A positive mindset can help sickle cell sufferers cope with the pain by reducing stress and anxiety, which can make the pain worse. Positive thinking can also help people focus on things they enjoy or find calming, distracting them from their distress.

Better mental health: Sickle cell disease can affect a person's mental health, leading to depression, anxiety, and other mental health problems. A positive mindset can help people with sickle cell disease feel more resilient and better able to cope with the challenges of the disease. It can also help reduce stress, which can improve overall mental health.

Improved quality of life: Sickle cell disease can affect a person's ability to work, attend school, and participate in activities they enjoy. A positive mindset can help sickle cell sufferers stay optimistic and maintain a positive outlook on life. This can help them stay engaged in activities they want, which can improve their quality of life.

Better relationships: A positive mindset can help sickle cell sufferers build better relationships with their families, friends, and healthcare providers. It can help them communicate their needs more effectively and improve their ability to collaborate with others to manage their condition.

Increased resilience: Sickle cell disease can be challenging to manage, and there may be times when a sickle cell sufferer feels overwhelmed. A positive mindset can help people with sickle cell disease become more resilient and better able to handle the ups and downs of the condition. This can help them maintain their motivation to manage the disease effectively and continue working toward their goals.

My advice

Travel if you can and be free. Sickle cell is not a death sentence. Just remember to take all your medication, drink enough water, try to avoid stress and infections, and prepare yourself when visiting countries with extreme temperatures. When travelling, ensure you have all the necessary vaccinations and medications. Make sure all your childhood vaccinations are up to date. Inform your GP or consultant about your travel plans, and make sure to stock up on medication. Be sensible and take chances when life permits you.

"If you can stay positive in a negative situation, you win".

Unknown

My Number One Supporters

When I was young, I still had both of my parents around. I attended the best schools in Ghana and always had both parents by my side, which made me feel like I could achieve anything. That's where I acquired my assertiveness. It may have compensated for my health issues, but I never felt different from other children. Instead, I felt superior and believed that my condition would not hinder me. My parents never made me feel like I had a disability, although at times, I felt my mother was overly involved in my life during my teenage and young adult years. I am immensely grateful for my upbringing and the parents that God blessed me with. This emphasises the Christian phrase, "God only gives you what you need and can handle." He provides just enough. I was fortunate to grow up in the best possible environment.

My dad loved me to bits, but in hindsight, I think he didn't want to deal with my "I don't take NO from anyone attitude." He will go above and beyond for me; I always get whatever I want from him. For instance, during my secondary school years, he arranged for me to attend Accra Girls School, a reputable institution in Accra. Patricia, my sibling, was already studying there, so it was convenient for me to gain admission through sibling privileges. However, one day I had an argument with

Patricia at school and impulsively decided I no longer wanted to be in the same school as her. I approached my dad and expressed my desire to switch to a different school solely because of Patricia. The next thing I knew, I was enrolled at St Mary's Catholic School, all thanks to my dad's influence. I truly appreciate having such an incredible father.

However, the story takes a bit of a twisted turn. When Patricia found out, she decided she didn't want to stay alone in Accra Girls. And guess what, readers? We ended up in the same school again. What a pointless exercise, but I went on to meet and make great friends there. We can't have it all, but in all circumstances, trust the process. I was fortunate to have my number one fans, but we can still make it even if our childhoods were different. Our experiences may not have been the same, but be thankful for whatever you had as a child. It makes us positive and less resentful if it isn't what we expected. Personally, I try not to stress about what I can't change. We need to believe that our parents and family did the best they could at that time. You can now change the narrative. Do not dwell or waste time on what you cannot change or reverse.

My advice

Always do what will make you happy while considering others. I am not a believer in 'Each man for himself, God for us all.' I believe we need to look after each other. Unfortunately, as sickle cell sufferers, we need that Number One FAN. Personally, I sometimes feel so much pain that I really don't want to get out of bed. I need my number one FAN or someone who understands my predicament to be there and show some love, care, and support. I am blessed to have my three girls and my amazing network of supportive friends. Their names would fill this page if I started writing about how blessed I have been to have all these people in my life. **Please, as a sickle cell sufferer, reach out to someone.**

"Many of life's failures are people who did not realise how close they were to success when they gave up."

Thomas A Edison.

The Trials and Tribulations

African people in the United Kingdom (UK) have encountered numerous obstacles. Despite being a minority community, they have made significant contributions to the UK's economy and culture. However, they still face various problems, including discrimination, lack of representation, and cultural barriers. This section will analyse the numerous issues that African people experience in the UK.

There are several challenges that African people face in the UK, which can be broadly classified into social, economic, and cultural challenges. Personally, I have encountered some key challenges...

Racism: I was called for an interview for a job with Selfridges. When I arrived, I was informed that the discussion had been postponed and that I would be notified of a new date as soon as possible. The reason became apparent when I noticed that I was the only black girl in the office. I believe my maiden name, Phillips, was the reason why I was invited for the interview, and obviously, my appearance was deceiving. However, this did not discourage me; it actually made me believe that I could make a difference, and I was determined not to let anyone make me feel inferior. I have faced discrimination throughout my life due to my medical condition, but no one is going to make me think less of myself.

Cultural barriers: I had to adapt to cultural norms and practices. My Christian faith was strong, and my mom always encouraged me to seek God first. Life in the UK meant that I sometimes had to work on Sundays, which was very different from what I was accustomed to in Ghana. This presented a challenge, and when I attempted to change my shift work so I could attend church, I realised I was constantly at odds with my line management, and I had to choose between paying my bills and going to church. It was a tough decision to make.

Another issue that African individuals experience in the UK is cultural boundaries. Africans struggle to assimilate into British culture due to differences in cultural norms and linguistic obstacles. One of the cultural hurdles that African people encounter is the disparity in schooling systems. African individuals often find it difficult to navigate the British school system, which can differ significantly from the education systems in their home countries. This can result in lower academic achievement and limited opportunities.

Another cultural hurdle that African people face is language barriers. English is not the native language for many Africans, making it challenging to communicate effectively and assimilate into British culture. Furthermore, linguistic challenges can hinder access to healthcare, education, and job opportunities.

African individuals also experience cultural difficulties in social interactions. British culture may differ greatly from African culture, leading to misunderstandings and social isolation. Additionally, Africans may feel pressure to conform to British society, resulting in a loss of cultural identity and a sense of displacement.

Economic challenges: I couldn't work till I had sorted my right to work in the UK, obtained an NI, and sought better job opportunities. In the 90s, I could access some benefits but not all. I was still determined to stand out and use all that was available.

- **Language barriers:** Language wasn't a barrier as I spoke English at home with my dad, so integrating into British society wasn't a challenge.

- **Immigration status:** Studying nursing gave me my legal right to work in the UK and access healthcare, education, and other essential services without fearing deportation.

- **Discrimination:** Discrimination is a critical issue faced by African people in the UK. Despite being a diversified country, racism and prejudice remain prominent in many regions of the UK. African people have reported facing racism and discrimination in numerous sectors, including education, work, housing, and healthcare.

- **Lack of Representation:** Another difficulty African people confront in the UK is the lack of representation. Despite being a significant minority in the UK, African people are underrepresented in various spheres of society, including politics, journalism, and business.

- **Institutional Barriers:** One of the institutional impediments that African people confront is the education system. African children are more likely to be excluded from school than their white peers, which can significantly influence their academic performance and prospects. Furthermore, African children are less likely to be labelled as gifted and talented, which can lead to a lack of access to opportunities.

Recommendations

To solve the issues experienced by African people in the UK, numerous proposals might be made:

- Enhance Representation

- Combat Discrimination:

- Promote Cultural Understanding:

- Expand Access to Opportunities:

- Address Institutional obstacles:

- Possible Counterarguments

Future Outlook

Looking ahead, several positive trends may help alleviate the issues faced by African people in the UK. As mentioned above, sickle cell sufferers are predominantly from Africa, so this directly or indirectly affects us. For instance, there has been a growing awareness of the need for diversity and inclusion in institutions, resulting in initiatives like the Race Equality Charter and the Race at Work Charter.

Conclusion

African people in the UK face numerous challenges, including discrimination, lack of representation, cultural barriers, and institutional obstacles. Most sickle cell sufferers are immigrants and may have personally experienced various forms of discrimination. This section is intended for anyone reading my book who wishes to make a difference. By addressing these issues, we can significantly improve the quality of life and opportunities for the future. Tackling these difficulties requires a collective effort from individuals, communities, and institutions.

Working together can help create a more inclusive and equitable society for everyone.

Migrating to a completely different continent can have a profound impact on individuals and families. This impact can manifest in a range of emotions, including anxiety, excitement, anticipation, and bewilderment. Personally, I experienced the challenge of leaving my friends and family behind and transitioning from familiar surroundings and places. My life has constantly worked, but I have always focused on the positives.

My advice

I had opportunities for personal growth and development while exposed to new ideas and perspectives in a new country. Despite my health challenges, I have also achieved fulfilling economic stability and, I presume, better living conditions. Seize any opportunity you may be faced with. Work with what you can change and leave the rest. I realised I couldn't fight all battles. I accepted, adapted, and changed what I could and left the rest to God. Stress is a trigger to sickle cell and other ailments. Avoid it at all costs.

> *"Everything negative – pressure, challenges -is all an opportunity for me to rise."*

Kobe Bryant

Passing The Borders into New Beginnings

My mother was the first to know that I may be staying in London longer than expected, but my dad was devastated when he found out I wasn't coming back anytime soon. My university prospects were going to be put on hold. Despite all these health challenges, I was determined to prove I could make it. My dad was so angry he initially refused to speak to me. After a year or so, I managed to go back and convinced him I was back for good. Little did he know I had a return ticket. I later called him when I got back and told him work had been requested, and I had returned. It was a blatant lie, but considering my dad's economic and social background, I was at risk of him asking me to be repatriated to Ghana. I wasn't keen to take that chance. By then, I had become adept at manoeuvring my way in the UK. Life was even better, and I had no intention of returning to Ghana.

I was just a 19-year-old girl with sickle cell, and there was no one apart from God when I started my life in the UK. My biological family was all back in Ghana, but God ensured I never lacked. It was difficult – don't get me wrong – but I was determined that my health wouldn't interfere with my goals. I convinced myself that sickle cell was a condition, not a life sentence. Like everyone else with a chronic disease, I could MAKE it; I will MAKE IT; I am MAKING it.

Living in the UK isolated me from my siblings, but I knew they were just a phone call away. I missed my family dearly, but my mother, may her soul rest in peace, constantly calling and checking up on me, made me more confident, and I never doubted what I was capable of.

She was always worried about my ill health, but "an African girl all alone in a foreign country" did not deter me. I believe my strong will and determination kept me alive and sane.

My advice

God will always watch over you; for the atheist, there is always a bigger force than you. Always believe in that philosophy and God/the universe won't let you down. I can't emphasise on "Live life to the fullest" enough. Change your mindset and believe you can do it when you put your mind to it.

"All you need is the plan and the courage to press on to your destinations."

Earl Nightingale

Can I ever be free of this Sickled Cell?

While bone marrow transplant currently remains the only cure for sickle cell disease, there exist additional treatments that can assist in managing the symptoms and effects of the condition. Recently, significant advancements have been achieved in the development of novel treatments for sickle cell disease. Among these treatments, a gene therapy approach utilising CRISPR-Cas9 technology to modify the DNA of the patient's stem cells has emerged as a particularly promising option.

A clinical trial was conducted in the United States, where several sickle cell patients received this gene therapy. The results were promising. The patients who received the treatment showed an increase in the production of healthy red blood cells and a decrease in the frequency and severity of sickle cell crises. However, the therapy is still in the early stages of development, and more research is needed to determine its safety and long-term effectiveness.

Also, another promising treatment for sickle cell disease is crizanlizumab, which was approved by the US Food and Drug Administration in 2019. This medication is known to reduce the frequency of crises, which can result in severe pain and organ damage. There are several treatments available that can help manage the symptoms and address any complications that may arise. The development of new medicines, such as gene therapy and crizanlizumab, provides hope for a future where sickle cell disease can be effectively treated and possibly even cured.

Treatment

As mentioned above, a blood and bone marrow transplant is currently the only cure for certain sickle cell patients. I can confirm that this treatment is being offered in the UK, but there are stringent processes in place to determine eligibility. It is worth mentioning this option to your consultant if you are considering it, as a successful transplant can lead to a cure for sickle cell. However, it is important to note that every medical procedure carries risks.

Babies with sickle cell disease may see a haematologist or a doctor specialising in blood ailments such as sickle cell disease. For babies, the first sickle cell disease visit should take place before eight weeks of age.

Medicines

Preventative medication for sickling Cells

Voxelotor reduces sickle cell crises in patients by inhibiting the formation of sickle-shaped red blood cells and their tendency to stick together. This mechanism helps minimise the breakdown of red blood cells, improves their overall health, reduces the risk of anaemia, and enhances blood flow to organs. It is important to note that Voxelotor is not recommended for individuals under the age of 12. It is taken orally in tablet form.

Medicine To Minimise Pain Crises

Crizanlizumab-tmca is licensed for adults and children that are 16 years old and older with sickle cell disease. The drug, delivered through an intravenous (IV) line in the vein, helps prevent blood cells from clinging to blood vessel walls and creating blood flow blockage, inflammation, and pain crises.

Medicine to decrease or prevent numerous problems

Hydroxyurea is an oral medication that minimises or avoids numerous consequences of sickle cell disease. It is a myelosuppressive agent known to increase foetal haemoglobin.

Medicine is prescribed to lower the chance of infection.

Penicillin administered twice daily can minimise children's likelihood of having a dangerous infection in the bloodstream. Newborns need to receive liquid penicillin.

Many healthcare practitioners will cease providing penicillin after a child reaches age 5. Antibiotics are normally prescribed throughout a sickle cell sufferer's life due to the high-risk factor. All patients who have undergone surgical spleen removal (known as a splenectomy) or have had a past infection with pneumococcus should take penicillin for the rest of their lives.

Medicine for the reduction of acute complications.

This treatment was approved by the FDA in 2017. This followed the publication of results from a study that showed L-glutamine supplementation resulted in a 25% reduction in pain crises and fewer hospitalizations over 48 weeks. It is taken orally as a powder and is thought to reduce oxidative stress damage.

Transfusions

Your doctor may recommend transfusion to treat and prevent specific sickle cell disease problems. Blood transfusions are being used more frequently over recent years. The aim is to dilute out sickle haemoglobin; this can be life-saving, for example, in acute chest syndrome, either as a top-up or an exchange.

These transfusions may include:

Acute transfusions treat problems that cause severe anaemia. Transfusions are given to sickle cell patients who have experienced an acute stroke in the past. A patient who has sickle cell disease frequently receives blood transfusions before surgery to prevent complications.

Red blood cell transfusions enhance the number of red blood cells and offer normal red blood cells that are more flexible than red blood cells with sickle haemoglobin. Exchange transfusion can also be given on a regular basis, typically every 4-6 weeks. This procedure involves administering 4-8 units of red blood cells while simultaneously removing approximately 70-80% of the patient's sickle blood. The process takes several hours and is performed in the day unit using an apheresis machine.

I am currently in this program; I have 8 bags of blood every 5 weeks. It can be lonely, always painful, terrifying, isolating, and daunting. I have had some setbacks with this program. My veins have been overused and have all disappeared (I have had 22 tries just to put a cannula into my vein during one hospital admission). That is how bad my veins are. I have a blood test 3 days before my exchange which is always excruciating. Imagine what I experience 3 days before the exchange. But that has helped me for almost 8 years now. This just reduces the previous hospital admissions via A & E.

Regular or continuous blood transfusions may help minimise the chances of future strokes in individuals who have had an acute stroke. Particularly in children with abnormal blood flow in the brain identified by transcranial Doppler screening. This screening test is offered to all children in England with sickle cell disease between the ages of 2 and 16 years. If the test shows abnormalities, a regular blood transfusion may be offered to maintain the sickle haemoglobin level below 30% in order to reduce the risk of stroke.

I used to receive blood transfusions, but not regularly, whenever I was pregnant.

Your healthcare practitioner may recommend transfusions to treat and prevent specific sickle cell disease problems such as acute chest syndromes.

Potential genetic therapy treatments

The National Health, Lung and Blood Institute NHLBI keep exploring ways that they can get a new treatment or a possible cure for sickle cell sufferers using genetic medicines. Let's all hope they get the funding and expertise needed to conclude these studies and help sickle cell sufferers all over the world.

Another type of pain one may experience is neuropathic pain, which manifests as shooting, burning, tingling, or numbness and can affect various body parts, such as the hands, feet, face, or trunk. I have been regularly taking Pregabalin to help manage my neuropathic pain. I frequently experience pins and needles in different parts of my body, but recently I have been experiencing shooting pain on my left side.

NSAIDs, such as ibuprofen, naproxen, and diclofenac, can

be effective for mild to moderate pain. However, their use may be limited due to potential adverse effects on the kidneys and stomach, particularly in patients with renal impairment or a history of gastric ulcers. Opioids, including tramadol, methadone, pethidine, and oxycodone, can be effective for moderate to severe pain. Nevertheless, their use may be restricted due to the potential for addiction, tolerance, respiratory depression, constipation, and other adverse effects.

Some non-pharmacological interventions for pain in sickle cell disease (SCD) include physical therapy, exercise, massage, acupuncture, and cognitive-behavioural therapy (CBT). Physical therapy and exercise can improve muscle strength, flexibility, and endurance while reducing stiffness and pain, although they may also increase fatigue. Based on personal experience, I believe that massage and acupuncture can promote relaxation, relax the muscles, and enhance blood flow to the affected areas.

I have never personally used cognitive-behavioural therapy (CBT), but based on professional knowledge, it can help patients to learn coping skills, improve communication with healthcare providers, and reduce negative thoughts and emotions that may exacerbate pain.

Supportive interventions for pain in SCD include hydration, oxygen therapy, blood transfusions, and surgery. Hydration can help prevent vaso-occlusion and reduce blood viscosity, making it less likely for sickled cells to form. This is something I am very good at—I drink a lot of water. It's also advisable to minimise alcohol consumption as it can cause dehydration. Oxygen therapy can increase tissue oxygenation and reduce ischemia, particularly during acute pain crises. When I am admitted to the hospital, I always receive oxygen therapy. Blood transfusions can increase the number of healthy red blood cells and reduce the proportion of sickled cells, thereby improving blood flow and reducing complications. Surgery can be used to correct bone deformities, remove damaged tissues, or transplant organs; however, it should be carefully considered and planned to avoid complications and exacerbation of pain.

The psychological and social impact of SCD can also contribute to the fatigue experienced by patients with anaemia. SCD can lead to a variety of emotional and social challenges, including anxiety, depression, social isolation, stigma, and discrimination. These factors can affect the patient's motivation, self-esteem, and quality of life. Moreover, they can also impact adherence to treatment, such as medication, hydration, and blood transfusions, thereby exacerbating the symptoms of anaemia and increasing the risk of complications.

The aim of the treatment is to correct the underlying cause, improve the oxygen-carrying capacity of the blood, and alleviate the symptoms of fatigue and other complications. This should be tailored to the individual needs and preferences of the patient, as well as the severity and type of anaemia. What may work for me would certainly not work for all. This is not a one-fit solution. All treatments should be carefully monitored to avoid complications like iron overload, transfusion reactions, and infections.

Dietary supplements, such as iron, folic acid, vitamin B12, and vitamin C, can also support the production and maintenance of healthy red blood cells and alleviate the symptoms of anaemia. I use these personally, and I believe they have all made a difference in my life at some stage of my journey. Vitamin D and black seed oil are also on my list.

Infections: Sickle cell disease can weaken the immune system, making people more susceptible to infections. The sickle-shaped cells are less flexible and more prone to rupture, blockage, and destruction, impairing the oxygen supply to the tissues and organs and causing various symptoms and complications. One of the complications of SCD is the weakening of the immune system, which makes people more susceptible to infections. The immune system is a complex network of cells, tissues, and organs that work together to defend the body against harmful microorganisms, such as bacteria, viruses, fungi, and parasites. The immune system can recognise and neutralise the invaders by various mechanisms, such as the production of antibodies, the activation of phagocytes, and the release of cytokines.

The immune system can also remember the previous encounters with the invaders and mount a faster and more robust response upon re-exposure. The immune system can be affected by various factors, such as age, genetics, nutrition, stress, and diseases. In SCD, the immune system can be weakened by several mechanisms, including damage to the spleen, the alteration of the white blood cells, and changes in the cytokine profile.

The spleen is an essential immune system organ that filters the blood and removes damaged or infected red blood cells, microorganisms, and debris. A damaged spleen can become less effective in filtering the blood and performing its other functions. When damaged, the spleen can also release red blood cells and their contents into the circulation, which can cause a systemic inflammatory response and further weaken the immune system.

My advice

I believe in miracles, and I know that one day we will be cured of these sickled cells. Please conduct research to discover new interventions. Consult with experts as they may have insights into new drugs and treatments. Inquire about eligibility for these options. Additionally, explore the resources available to you at present and determine how you can manage your symptoms effectively. The UK is fortunate to have a national blood transfusion service; therefore, supplies of blood are available. However, more donors are needed, especially those from ethnic minority communities. Please encourage friends and family members to donate blood.

Some UK hospitals offer inpatient interventions such as yoga, virtual reality, and acupuncture, which are known to decrease pain scale scores. Outpatient therapies could include cognitive-behavioural therapy, massage therapy, and guided imagery, which are likely to increase pain tolerability and decrease pain scale scores. Progressive relaxation techniques, self-hypnosis, and spiritual support are also often used.

Find out what works best for you. Consider joining sickle cell clubs to meet new people and engage in activities such as spas, holidays and exercises suitable for your abilities.

"Nurturing yourself is not selfish – it's essential to your survival and your well-being."

Renee Peterson Trudeau

Deal with it

Managing infections in SCD can be challenging and requires a multidisciplinary approach. The administration should aim to prevent the infections, identify and diagnose the diseases early, treat the infections effectively, and avoid the complications of the conditions. Various strategies, such as vaccination, prevention, and hygiene can prevent infections. The vaccination can protect the patient from specific diseases more common in SCD, such as pneumococcal, meningococcal, and influenza.

Hygiene can reduce exposure to microorganisms, such as hand washing, avoiding contact with sick people, and avoiding crowded places.

Anxiety is characterised by excessive worry and fear, which can be related to the illness, its treatment, or its impact on daily life. Stress can cause physical symptoms such as restlessness, irritability, and muscle tension. It can also impact a person's ability to manage illness, adhere to treatment, and maintain healthy behaviours. Chronic disease can also lead to other mental health conditions, such as Post-Traumatic Stress Disorder (PTSD) and adjustment disorder. I have experienced some terrible hospital stays and believe this could have easily led to PTSD, compounded with the pain I was experiencing then.

I know it is easy for me to say, but avoiding adjustment disorder at all costs is paramount to one's well-being. This occurs when a person struggles to cope with a significant life change, such as a chronic illness diagnosis and can cause symptoms such as anxiety, depression, and difficulty adjusting to the new situation. Please remember sickle cell is not going anywhere unless you have a bone marrow transplant; the sooner you embrace it, the better. I must be honest: I properly embraced my condition when I worked on PPW4; it was the best thing I ever did. I started living life. Living with a chronic illness can also impact a person's relationships with others. I try to explain this to friends and family around me, just so they don't think I am being awkward. I need them to understand me when I act in certain ways.

Chronic disease can require significant lifestyle changes, such as a restricted diet, frequent medical appointments, and reduced physical activity. These changes can be challenging for the person living with the illness and their family and friends. Managing a chronic disease can lead to conflicts and strain on relationships, which further impacts a person's mental health. This is where you need someone to love you unconditionally, not just saying it but also acting it. The action certainly speaks louder than words.

Living with a chronic illness can also impact a person's

social life. The physical and emotional symptoms of chronic illness can limit their ability to participate in social activities, including sports, hobbies, and gatherings with friends and family. This isolation can further affect their mental health and overall well-being. Therefore, I call upon friends and family to understand our situation. Dealing with chronic pain can be exhausting, tiring, and draining. We did not choose to be in this condition, so I kindly ask for your understanding and cooperation in supporting us.

There are several strategies that people living with chronic illness can use to manage their mental health. One method is to seek support from a mental health professional, such as a therapist or counsellor. A mental health professional can provide coping strategies and emotional support to help manage the stress and emotional challenges of living with a chronic illness. Another method is to connect with others who are living with similar conditions. Support groups can provide emotional support and practical advice on managing symptoms and navigating the healthcare system. Support groups can also help reduce feelings of isolation and improve social connections.

Maintaining healthy habits such as exercise, a balanced diet, and adequate sleep can also help manage mental health symptoms. Exercise has been shown to reduce symptoms of depression and anxiety and improve physical health. A balanced diet can help manage symptoms such as fatigue, while adequate sleep can improve mood and cognitive function. Communicating openly with healthcare providers about mental health symptoms is also essential. Healthcare providers can provide referrals to mental health professionals and may be able to adjust treatment plans to better manage mental health symptoms.

Living with a chronic illness can be challenging, but it is essential to prioritise mental health and well-being. Managing mental health symptoms can improve the overall quality of life and help individuals better manage their illnesses. It is also important to remember that seeking help for mental health issues is a sign of strength and courage and can lead to better outcomes in both psychological and physical health.

In addition to seeking support and managing mental health symptoms, several steps can be taken to minimise the impact of chronic illness on work and employment. Chronic disease can affect a person's ability to work in several ways, such as physical limitations, fatigue, and pain. It can also impact a person's cognitive skills, such as memory, concentration, and decision-making. One strategy to manage the impact of chronic illness on work is to communicate openly with employers and colleagues. This may involve discussing accommodations such as flexible work hours, modified duties, or assistive technology to help manage physical limitations. It may also include communicating the impact of fatigue and cognitive difficulties on work performance and seeking colleague support.

Another strategy is to prioritise self-care and work-life balance. This may involve taking breaks throughout the workday to rest or manage symptoms, such as stretching or taking medication. It may also include taking time off work to control symptoms or attend medical appointments. Maintaining a balanced lifestyle that includes regular exercise, healthy eating, and adequate sleep can also help manage symptoms and improve work performance. It is also important to understand legal protections for employees with chronic illnesses.

Living with a chronic illness can be challenging, but managing symptoms and maintaining a fulfilling life is possible. Prioritising mental health, seeking support, and managing the impact of chronic illness on work can help individuals with chronic disease preserve a sense of control and empowerment in their lives. With the proper support, resources, and self-care strategies, it is possible to thrive despite the challenges of chronic illness.

Sickle cell disease can significantly burden family members. I know this firsthand, as I see how my children are constantly concerned about me and believe they have to take care of me all the time.

Last year on the 3rd of August 2022, I was leaving a house in Croydon, and when I stepped on the pavement, the slab gave way underneath me. I sustained this huge laceration beneath my right knee. It was the second most challenging time of my life. [By the way, if you are wondering what the first most challenging time was, it was losing my mum two years ago.] I was rushed to the hospital in a friend's car as the hospital said it would take 55 minutes for an ambulance to come to me.

I was bleeding profusely and had to have my leg in a black bag tied tightly to minimise the bleeding. Obviously, the support from my friends was next to none. This pain was the worst type of pain I had ever experienced, apart from labour, of course. I was prepared for surgery that evening, but there was a delay due to the input of the sickle cell consultant. They needed to ensure it was safe to operate on me; as you may be aware, it can be dangerous to operate on sickle cell sufferers due to the risk of complications caused by low levels of oxygen during surgery. By then, I was suffering from a full-blown crisis and was feeling all sorts of pain at that time. I had also lost a significant amount of blood, which made the whole surgery riskier for me.

Kalisha was with me when my friend was driving me to the hospital, and Donnika stayed with me the entire night until I was taken to the operating theatre. She remained by my side, and we all prayed together over the phone before I went in for surgery.

Even little Alexia, the baby, was praying for me during this time. The support from my family was truly incredible.

I realise the impact of my condition, and of course, sickle cell disease extends well beyond the individual with the ailment. My family members were affected in different ways. Although this injury was not a direct result of sickle cell, it triggered a crisis. I stayed in the hospital under the care of both the orthopaedic and haematology teams.

The emotional impact of sickle cell illness on families can be severe. Parents of children with SCD may experience feelings of shame or a sense of responsibility for passing on the genetic mutation that causes the disease. Although my mom never explicitly told me, I could sense that she always felt she had to do more for me than for my siblings. Perhaps it was due to the reason mentioned earlier. Additionally, they may feel overwhelmed by the responsibilities of caring for a child with a chronic illness, including managing discomfort and frequent hospitalisations. I observed this in a few of my friends who have children with sickle cell disease.

Siblings of children with SCD may also experience emotional issues. In my case, my siblings thought I was being treated with favouritism, but I now realise it was more out of pity, sympathy, and perhaps even guilt. I believe they felt overshadowed by the constant attention and support I was receiving. Unfortunately, these feelings can have an impact on their self-esteem, relationships with family members, and overall well-being. I am sharing this because I want parents to be aware of the potential impact on other children in the family. This could even lead to jealousy or sibling rivalry if not dealt with in a tactful manner. Families need to understand the complexity and implications of having a child with a disability and focus on each individual in a special way. Just as the body needs all its limbs to function properly, we must take care of every member for the family unit to remain intact and not fall apart.

Social Impact - Sickle cell illness can have a significant social impact on families. Individuals with SCD may face prejudice or stigma related to their disease, resulting in social isolation and exclusion. This can be especially challenging for children who are trying to make friends and participate in activities. Family members may also experience social isolation as they care for a loved one with SCD. The responsibilities of caregiving can consume time and limit opportunities to participate in social events or pursue personal interests. Additionally, the financial strain of caring for a loved one with a chronic disease can restrict the family's ability to engage in activities or travel.

Financial impact - the burden of sickle cell disease on families can be enormous. Individuals with SCD require regular medical care, including hospitalisations, medicines, and specialised therapies. The expense of these therapies can be significant, particularly for families who do not have appropriate health insurance or who reside in countries without universal healthcare. The cost of caring for a child with SCD can significantly affect the financial stability of the family. Parents may need to take time off from work to care for their children or limit their work hours to attend medical visits. This might lead to a loss of income and place a financial burden on the family.

Practical Impact - Sickle cell illness can also have practical ramifications for families. Individuals with SCD may require frequent medical appointments, hospitalisations, and specialised therapies, which can be time-consuming and disruptive to everyday activities. Parents may need to take time off from work to attend medical appointments or provide care for their children, which might impair their ability to maintain employment or pursue educational opportunities.

Additionally, individuals with SCD may face limitations in their physical abilities, such as difficulties in participating in strenuous activities or sports. This might impact their capacity to engage in school or community activities and may lead to feelings of loneliness or exclusion.

Coping Strategies

Despite the many obstacles connected with sickle cell disease, there are ways that families may employ to manage the emotional, social, economic, and practical consequences of the condition. Dynamic coping tactics may include requesting help from friends, family members, or mental health specialists. It might be helpful for parents to connect with other parents of children with SCD to exchange experiences and coping skills. Siblings may benefit from support groups or individual treatment to help them process their feelings and enhance their self-esteem.

Social coping methods may involve finding ways to engage in activities that meet the requirements of the individual with SCD. For example, parents may seek out social events that are accessible or discover methods to adjust actions to make them more inclusive. It may also be helpful for families to connect with advocacy groups or organisations that support persons with SCD and their families.

Financial coping tactics may involve receiving financial aid through government programs or non-profit groups. It can also be helpful for families to construct a budget and financial plan that considers the expense of medical treatment and caring duties. Parents may also explore flexible work arrangements or find methods to create more money to cover the cost of caring for their child.

Practical coping methods may include a regimen incorporating medical visits and caregiving obligations. Parents should prioritise self-care and seek respite care to alleviate the parenting load. Additionally, parents may explore finding ways to adapt activities to make them more accessible for their child with SCD, such as locating adapted sports programs or changing physical activities to meet their child's needs. I haven't had the privilege of caring for a child with sickle cell disease, so I can only imagine how daunting it must be. Especially seeing your child in pain but unable to alleviate the distress.

Undeniably, sickle cell illness profoundly impacts families, resulting in emotional, social, economic, and practical repercussions. It is crucial for families to seek assistance and learn coping mechanisms to effectively manage the challenges associated with the disease. By finding strategies to adapt to the needs of the individual with SCD and prioritising self-care, families can minimise the stress of the illness and enhance their overall well-being. Additionally, advocacy and awareness activities can help reduce the stigma and prejudice associated with SCD, improving social and emotional outcomes for individuals with the disorder and their families.

Finances: The cost of treating sickle cell disease can be significant, leading to financial stress for individuals and families. Overall, sickle cell disease can impact a person's quality of life, educational and employment opportunities, and relationships with family and friends. Unfortunately, we need access to comprehensive care and support to manage the challenges associated with the condition.

The significant financial burden of sickle cell disease is the expense of medical treatment. Individuals with SCD require regular medical checkups, hospitalisations, and specific therapies, such as blood transfusions and bone marrow transplants.

In addition to medical expenditures, patients with SCD may also require specific equipment, such as mobility assistance, oxygen tanks, or adapted beds. These fees can mount up rapidly and may not be covered by NHS. I consider myself fortunate to be in the UK, where most of these expenses are covered, except for the cost of my medicines.

Sickle cell sufferers may face a reduced capacity to work or attend school due to the numerous medical appointments, hospitalisations, and so on. I can attest to this; however, I believe we can always look at the positive side. Life is not a race; you can achieve things at your own pace. This can be particularly problematic for families without appropriate social safety nets or those who do not have access to disability payments.

Parents may need to take time off from work to care for their children or reduce their work hours to attend medical visits. This can result in a loss of income and create a financial burden for the entire family. However, I am a strong believer in taking care of our own. We must come together and manage as best we can.

The financial stress and worry associated with SCD can affect one's mental health and overall well-being. Unfortunately, I can't escape this aspect of my life. I tend to worry, and most of my friends reinforce this behaviour. The irony is that worry only intensifies the symptoms of SCD, so it becomes pointless. As a Christian, I focus on the Bible and its verses to help me manage my stress.

My Advice

It would be beneficial to create a budget and financial plan that takes into account all expenses, including medical treatments and so on. This will help individuals and families organise their expenditures and minimise unnecessary costs. Additionally, it will aid in planning for future expenses and building up resources to cover unforeseen bills.

Individuals and families may also consider exploring flexible employment arrangements or finding ways to generate additional income to cover the costs associated with caring for their child with SCD. This could involve working from home, pursuing part-time employment, or starting a side business. It is also essential for individuals and families to prioritise self-care, including mental health treatment.

Seeking counselling or therapy can assist individuals in managing the financial stress and concerns associated with SCD. It can also help individuals develop strategies to effectively manage their condition and improve their overall well-being.

Additionally, advocacy and awareness initiatives can help eliminate the stigma and discrimination associated with SCD, leading to improved social and emotional outcomes for individuals with the disorder and their families. By raising awareness about the economic impact of SCD, we can help reduce the burden on individuals and families and enhance their overall quality of life.

Ten haemoglobinopathy centres were set up in the UK, with four based in London. These are large specialist centres that provide both clinical care and are responsible for advising and educating clinicians and patients.

Sickle cell care is also available in England, but in smaller, more local hospitals through Specialist Haemoglobinopathy teams.

New 24/7 Hyper Acute Units are being established initially in London and Manchester. In these specially staffed units, patients will be able to receive immediate pain care from knowledgeable clinicians and avoid waiting in A&E.

My Conclusion

Sickle cell disease can substantially influence an individual's life. We have to be positive and embrace the condition. It is here to stay, and the sooner one finds ways to manage the condition, the better.

We must understand the severity of pain in order to reduce unnecessary suffering. When you are in pain, use the medication provided, and please do not dwell on the stigma surrounding the use of opioids for pain management. Unfortunately, some healthcare professionals incorrectly assume that individuals with sickle cell disease are more prone to opioid addiction. This misconception can lead to under-treatment of pain and unnecessary suffering.

Tackling social determinants of health, such as poverty, racism, and discrimination, can impact the health outcomes of people with sickle cell disease. Joining charities, donations, and research can profoundly help the individual, their family and the medical industry.

Overall, Healthcare professionals need to receive education and training about sickle cell disease and for increased awareness and funding for research in this field.

Here are some of the most common misconceptions about SCD:

Sickle cell disease only affects people of African descent: While sickle cell disease is more common in people of African descent, it can affect people of any race or ethnicity. It is also found in people of Mediterranean, Middle Eastern, and Indian descent.

Sickle cell disease is contagious: Sickle cell disease is not infectious and cannot be transmitted from one person to another.

Sickle cell disease only affects red blood cells: While sickle cell disease primarily affects red blood cells, it can also cause damage to other organs and tissues in the body.

Sickle cell disease is a death sentence: While sickle cell disease can be a severe condition, with proper medical care and management, people with sickle cell disease can live long and productive lives.

People with sickle cell disease are constantly in pain: While pain is a common symptom of sickle cell disease, not all people with the condition experience pain all the time. The severity and frequency of pain can vary significantly from person to person.

Sickle cell trait is the same as sickle cell disease: Sickle cell trait differs from sickle cell disease. People with sickle cell trait have one copy of the sickle cell gene and are generally healthy. In contrast, people with sickle cell disease have two copies and can experience various symptoms and complications.

Living with sickle cell disease in Africa can be challenging due to various factors, highlighting the need for increased awareness, research, and access to care and support in the region. I faced numerous challenges when I gave a birth to my first daughter at the age of 23. As I didn't have British citizenship, there were many obstacles to overcome. I started my nursing diploma in 1999 and successfully completed it in 2001 when my daughter was five years old. I was a single mother when I embarked on the course, facing numerous challenges, including concerns about my health. In 2002, I got married, and subsequently, we had two daughters. The second was born in 2003, and the third in 2007. Unfortunately, in 2020, divorce proceedings were initiated due to what I perceived as the ultimate betrayal. However, I believe that this was part of God's plan for my life.

My mother, who has been my counsellor, confidant, advisor, a shoulder to cry on, died on 24th May 2021. It's a terrible blow for me. I then had a severe injury while walking on the pavement, which caved in, and I suffered extensive ulceration below my right knee in 2022. I was rushed to the hospital, where I was taken to the theatre, hospitalised for 21 days, and in a cast for another couple of weeks, immobile with all the other challenges. I have had my fair share of disasters. I also completed my Master's (MBA) in 2019 while going through the divorce.

"Stay positive. Better days are on their way."

Unknown

My Reliable Resources

Links

- https://www.sicklecellsociety.org/

- https://www.epsom-sthelier.nhs.uk/haematology

- https://www.sicklecellsociety.org

- https://www.kch.nhs.uk/wp-content/uploads/2023/02/3324-Haematology-Red-Cell-Services_v15_FINAL.pdf

My medication

- Vitamin D

- Black seed oil

- Glucosamine Sulphate

- Magnesium oral tablets

- Feroglobin

- Magnesium Oil

- Vitamin C

- 5kind Active Gel 300ml – joint and muscle

My books

- The Bible

- Secrets

- Acts of Faith (Iyanla Vanzant)

- Rich Dad Poor Dad

- The Power of a Praying Woman

- The Power of a Praying Mother

- The Way of Wisdom

- Clarity & Connection

Alternative methods

- Shiatsu neck messager

- Kaspera-Aromatherapy-Essential-Natural-Mindfulness

- Inspiration Cushion cover

- Theraflow Foot Massager

- Antistress Cube

- Mindfulness Self Care

- Massage cream

- Bath Salts

Useful Journals

- Roth, M., Krystal, J., Manwani, D., Driscoll, C. and Ricafort, R. (2012). Stem Cell Transplant for Children with Sickle Cell Anemia: Parent and Patient Interest. *Biology of Blood and Marrow Transplantation*, 18(11), pp.1709–1715. doi: https://doi.org/10.1016/j.bbmt.2012.05.013.

- https://www.cdc.gov/ncbddd/sicklecell/features/stories-of-sickle-cell.html#print

- Chou, S. T., Evans, P., Vege, S., Coleman, S. L., Friedman, D. F., Keller, M., et al. (2018). RH genotype matching for transfusion support in sickle cell disease. *Blood* 132, 1198–1207. doi: 10.1182/blood-2018-05-851360

- Hoppe, C., Jacob, E., Styles, L., Kuypers, F., Larkin, S. and Vichinsky, E., (2017). Simvastatin reduces vaso-occlusive pain in sickle cell anaemia: a pilot efficacy trial. *British journal of haematology*, *177*(4), pp.620-629.

- https://www.addtoany.com/share#url=https%3A%2F%2Fwww.nhlbi.nih.gov%2Fhealth%2Fsickle-cell-disease&title=What%20Is%20Sickle%20Cell%20Disease%3F

Useful numbers

- **Emergency services UK   999/112**

- **Sickle cell society**   _____

- **Hospital number**   _____

- **Ward direct number**   _____

- **Consultant Number/bleep** _____

- **Careers Number**   _____

- **My next of kin**   _____

- **Day Unit number**   _____

Printed in Great Britain
by Amazon

29152419R00056